Hamida Aziz

Deep, blue and deadly

An eco-thriller set in the Maldives

W0348114

mit Hör-CD

Ernst Klett Verlag
Stuttgart · Leipzig

1. Auflage 1 5 4 3 2 1 | 2013 12 11 10 09

Alle Drucke dieser Auflage sind unverändert und können im Unterricht nebeneinander verwendet werden. Die letzten Zahlen bezeichnen jeweils die Auflage und das Jahr des Druckes.
Das Werk und seine Teile sind urheberrechtlich geschützt. Jede Nutzung in anderen als den gesetzlich zugelassenen Fällen bedarf der vorherigen schriftlichen Einwilligung des Verlages. Hinweis zu § 52 a UrhG: Weder das Werk noch seine Teile dürfen ohne eine solche Einwilligung eingescannt und in ein Netzwerk eingestellt werden. Dies gilt auch für Intranets von Schulen und sonstigen Bildungseinrichtungen.
Fotomechanische Wiedergabe nur mit Genehmigung des Verlages.

© Ernst Klett Verlag GmbH, Stuttgart 2009. Alle Rechte vorbehalten.
www.klett.de

Illustrationen: David Norman, Meerbusch
Bildquellen: 5.1 iStockphoto (Cornelis Opstal), Calgary, Alberta; 5.2 shutterstock (Miguel Angel Salinas Salinas), New York, NY; 41.1 Bilderberg (Reinhard Dirscherl), Hamburg; 41.2 iStockphoto (Michael Wicks), Calgary, Alberta; 41.3 iStockphoto (Heike Loos), Calgary, Alberta; 41.4 iStockphoto (Dave Bluck), Calgary, Alberta

Druck: Gulde-Druck GmbH, Tübingen
Printed in Germany.
ISBN 978-3-12-547595-3

9 783125 475953

For Samira,
for never letting daughterly enthusiasm cloud her critical eye.

Contents

Before you read the story

1 The title and the cover

a) *What hints do you get about the story from the title and the picture on the cover?*

b) *Why does the girl in the picture look so scared? What has she just seen? What do you think?*

2 Eco-thrillers[1]

a) *Think of eco-thrillers (books or films) you know. What are they about?*

b) *Now find the correct definition. An eco-thriller …*

1. … has characters who are all Green Corps members.
2. … is kind of mystery to do with the environment.
3. … is always about life under the sea.
4. … is a fantasy or horror story with animals.

3 Islands in paradise?

a) *Look at the map on page 6 and say where the Maldives are in relation to India. And where are they in relation to Europe? Not sure? Check in an atlas[1].*

b) *What could the main industry be in the Maldives: fishing, building, tourism, farming …? Why do you think this?*

c) *Look up 'atolls[3]' on the Internet. Complete the sentences.*

1. An atoll is an island made of *(ice/coral/rocks)*.
2. It forms a ring around water in the *(sea/park/lake)*.
3. The name comes from the *(French/Dhivehi/Turkish)* word 'atholhu'.

1 **eco-thriller** [ˈiːkəʊˌθrɪlə] Umweltkrimi • 2 **atlas** [ˈætləs] Atlas • 3 **atoll** [ˈætɒl]

4. An atoll has small islands and *(reefs/mountains/deserts)*.
5. The atoll with the most islands is in *(Hawaii/the British Isles/the Maldives)*.

4 Diving

a) *Look at the words below which have to do with diving.*

buddy • wetsuit • fin • mask • tank • jacket • torch

b) *Look at the photo and find the words from the box above. (Match each one with the right number). Check in a dictionary.*

c) *Try to guess what these international diving signals mean:*

You OK? • Let's go up. • Let's go down. • I need help!

d) *Would you like to go diving? Say why/why not.*

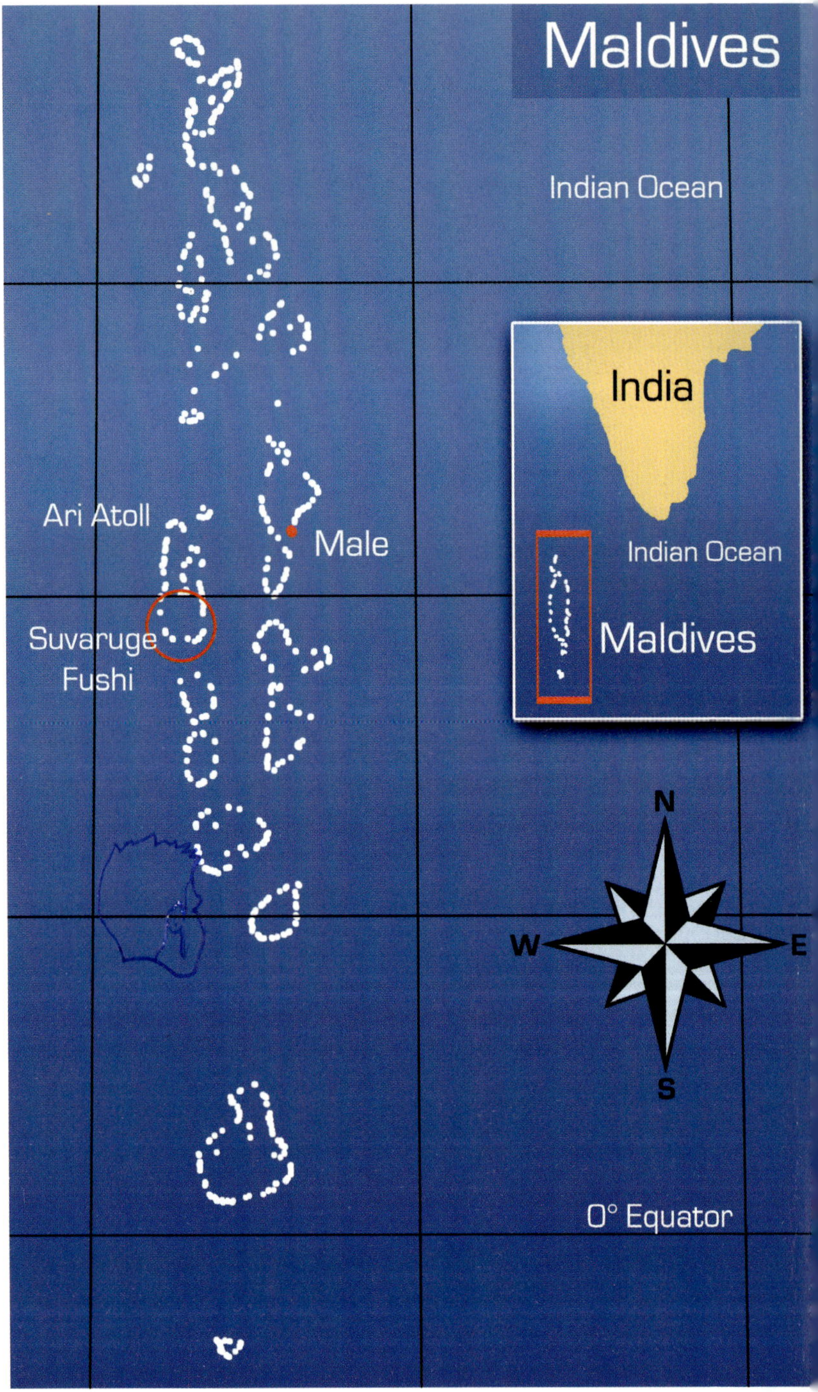

Maldives
Indian Ocean
India
Indian Ocean
Maldives
Ari Atoll
Male
Suvaruge
Fushi
N
W
E
S
0° Equator

Part 1 Suvaruge Fushi

Amber and Joel stepped out of the cool **shade** of their 'water villa' into the sunlight. It was a perfect evening. The sun hung low over a calm but glowing sea. At the point, where the sea touched land, the water broke **gently** in tiny, little waves on the pristine, white sands. Then silently the **equatorial** sun just dropped into the water, or so it **seemed**, and suddenly it was night. At that moment, the torches in the restaurant gardens came on like flares, as if **activated** by the sun disappearing.

As Amber and Joel left the walkway, which offered the only link between the villas and the island, Amber said,

"Wow, it's fantastic here. This island is my idea of paradise on Earth! Joel, I'm so glad this group wasn't already full when we **booked** it in Sydney."

"Yeah, me, too," said Joel, "although our idea of 'paradise on Earth' isn't all that original: The island isn't called 'Suvaruge Fushi' for nothing. The name is **Dhivehi**, the official language of the Maldives, and it means …"

"Paradise Island, I guess?" laughed Amber.

By now Joel and Amber had reached the table where the three other young Australians who shared their villa – Zach, **Hayley** and Connor – were also sitting.

"Hi, you two," said Zach. "Did I just hear the word 'paradise'? Well, that's exactly our feeling about the place, you know. I've been on a lot of diving holidays, but the hotel and scenery here are the best by far!"

"Yes, let's hope the scenery below water is as good as it is above," added Connor.

"Oh, come on, Con, it's only our first day here!" said Hayley. "I thought our first dive on the inner reef was great this afternoon. I wish I had a digital underwater camera like yours, Amber! The reef life down there is out of this world."

Suvaruge Fushi ['su:vʌru:gə ˌfu:ʃi] erfundener Name einer Insel • 1 **shade** [ʃeɪd] Schatten, Farbton • 4 **gently** ['dʒentli] sanft • 6 **equatorial** [ˌekwə'tɔ:riəl] äquatorial, tief stehend • 7 **seemed** [si:md] schien • 9 **to activate** ['æktɪveɪt] *hier:* anzünden • 14 **to book** [bʊk] buchen • 17 **Dhivehi** [dɪ'veɪhi] Sprache der Bevölkerung der Malediven • 22 **Hayley** ['heɪli] weibl. Vorname

“Yeah, you’re too right. But the camera isn’t exactly mine: It belongs to our diving club back in Sydney,” said Amber. “Well, I got lots of good photos with it today, but I haven’t downloaded them onto my laptop yet. I must show you all my shots of those spectacular white-face **butterfly fish**.”

“What?” Joel moaned, trying to look disappointed. “And I thought all those photos that you took were of *me*!”

“No chance, Joel. At least not in the underwater world, right?” said Zach and **winked** at Amber. Then he added, “Did you get any photos of Abu? I believe our dive instructor made a real impression on Hayley, eh?”

“Zach, don’t be silly!” said Hayley, but her face started to turn red. “What I said was: Abu seems OK to me.”

Joel rescued Hayley by getting up, “I don’t know about you, but I’m so hungry, I could eat a horse! Let’s see what the buffet here has to offer!”

They were enjoying their meal when the waiter brought them some more drinks. The name on his shirt said ‘**Faruq**’.

“Excuse me, Faruq,” said Amber. “This fish curry is so tasty! Could you tell me what it’s called, please?”

5 **butterfly fish** [ˈbʌtəflaɪ ˌfɪʃ] eine Art Korallenfisch • 9 **to wink** [wɪŋk] zwinkern • 19 **Faruq** [fəˈruːk] männl. Vorname

"Yes, of course, we call it '**kirugarudhiya**' – yellow coconut curry," the waiter replied with a smile.

"So, what fish is in it? It's a real dream. It must be fresh from the fishermen's net!" suggested Joel.

"Er ... well, it's ... um ... yes, it's red snapper. That's what you call it in English, I think ..." said the waiter, as he put a bottle of water on the table.

"Ah," said Joel, "we've got red snappers in Australia, too. We call them 'Jacks', I can't tell you why! But Amber is right, this is great stuff. I think I'll go and get some more."

"Better than a horse, eh?" joked Zach. "But Joel, watch out, or you'll be as heavy as lead on the dive tomorrow, and we'll just have to leave you down in the deep, blue sea!"

• • •

The next morning Zach, Joel and Amber were the first to get to Abu's boat.

"G'day to you, **Abubakar**!" said Zach, as he climbed on board. "Where are we diving today?"

"Hi, there. So you're all up nice and early?" smiled Abu, helping the divers with their equipment. "That's good. We're exploring the other side of the reef this morning. I'd like you to meet a good friend! Let's hope Napoleon is there today."

Righty-ho, thought Amber, a friend called Napoleon who maybe fishes out there? She started to ask, but Abu went on,

"Just wait until we get there," he said, and then added, "Zach, you've done over fifty dives, so you can be dive leader for your two **buddies**. I'll be with Connor and Hayley. Faruq is coming with us this morning, so he'll stay on the boat."

Just then Faruq arrived with the other two divers and soon they were off. Ten minutes later Abu stopped the boat.

1 **kirugarudhiya** [ˌki:ru:gʌru:ˈdi:jɑ:] • 16 **Abubakar** [ˌʌbu:ˈbʌkʌr] männl. Vorname • 23 **Righty-ho** [ˌraɪti ˈhəʊ] Alles klar • 28 **buddy** [ˈbʌdi] Tauchbegleiter/-in

The water was clear, warm and inviting, as it was all around the islands of the Maldives. Amber thought of Abu's 'good friend', but there were no other boats in sight. She put her wetsuit on. Each time she smelled its rubber, it brought back fantastic pictures of earlier dives. So, as always, she felt really excited before the big jump down.

They all checked the air in their tanks again, set their dive computers and got their fins on.

"I know, you're all good divers," started Abu as he **spat** into his mask and washed it out with some sea water, "but there's a current down there so it'll **move us along** a bit. Well, that's no problem, but I want you all to pivot at around ten metres. All of you give me the OK and then just follow me. And remember *never* touch the coral reef!"

• • •

They all dived. Amber loved the calm feeling as she let out her breath and fell down – down into the underwater world. The water here was at first the soft blue of an early morning sky, but took on different shades of blues and greens as she moved through it. Joel was in front of her, but he'd dropped a bit deeper. He's too fast, she thought. She let some air out of her jacket and met him half way as he came up to meet the others.

On the reef a **myriad of** brilliant life forms – corals, sponges, fish and plants – met their eyes. As they planned, the divers followed Abu until they came to a kind of **wide gap** in the reef. Amber was taking some photos when, **out of the blue**, a big, majestic fish swam over to Abu. It was about a metre long. It had wild, orange eyes but seemed gentle enough. Suddenly it held out its **fin**. Abu took it and **stroked** the fish with his other hand. Amber got a shot just in the right time! So *this* is Abu's friend Napoleon, she thought.

9 **spat** [spæt] spuckte • 11 **move along** [ˌmuːv əˈlɒŋ] *hier:* mitreißen • 23 **myriad of** [ˈmɪriəd ɒv] unzählige • 26 **wide** [waɪd] breit • 26 **gap** [gæp] Loch • 27 **out of the blue** [ˌaʊt əv ðə ˈbluː] plötzlich • 29 **fin** [fɪn] Flosse • 30 **to stroke** [strəʊk] streicheln

Napoleon then came over to the other divers and touched them with his nose as if he wanted to play. Together with this big, friendly fish they explored the reef. After another ten minutes or so Abu gave the **thumbs-up** signal – time to swim up again slowly.

Back on the boat, Faruq gave each diver half a coconut full of coconut water to wash the salt out of their mouths.

Zach turned to Abu, "Glad to meet your friend, Napoleon. Those **Napoleon wrasses** are great creatures. I've read about them, but this is the first one that I've ever met!"

"Are there lots of them out here?" asked Amber, who had started to write about the dive in her logbook.

"No, the Napoleon wrasse is on the 'red list'," said Faruq. "That means you shouldn't catch it. But tell that to those rich idiots who pay up to $400 just to eat Napoleon's lips!"

Amber finished her logbook entry with Faruq's last sentence just as they reached Suvaruge Fushi.

4 **thumbs-up** [θʌmz‿ˈʌp] Zeichen zum Auftauchen • 9 **Napoleon wrasse** [nəˈpəʊliən ˌræs] Napoleon-Lippfisch

Part 2 Islanders: Zahra

It was just before dawn. On the fishing island where Faruq's family lived his twin sister, Zahra, was packing her dad's breakfast. When the call for prayers sounded across the village, Zahra finished her work quickly and joined her parents. After that she and her dad left the island in his boat.

"If this goes on much longer, how will I feed the family?" Mr **Latif** said, more to himself than to his daughter.

"Who do you think is doing this?" asked Zahra. "It can't be anyone from our village ..."

"I don't know. We aren't fishing in the area any more. We have to go out quite far. But hotels still won't buy our fish. Just imagine: Their menus say 'fresh, local fish'. And there's nothing we can do!" Mr Latif **shook** his head sadly.

"Except catch those **wicked** people," suggested Zahra.

"Not so easy, I'm afraid," said her dad. "But listen, Zahra, I'll take you to Suvaruge Fushi before I go and pick up my **baitfish**. I must talk to the other fishermen – maybe they know more ..."

"OK, Dad," answered Zahra, with a heavy heart. Then she added, "I'm sure Faruq will be happy for some help."

By the time Zahra got out of the boat, the sun was coming up. She waved goodbye to her dad and walked along the beach. In the early morning light she could see Faruq. He was standing alone on the sands with his hands on his hips. He was looking out over the ocean. Next to him was a big wheelbarrow, more than half full of fish.

"Oh, my God! So many!" whispered Zahra. "It's good that Dad didn't see them – he'd be even more upset. Come on, Faruq, let me help you. We must get them away from here before the hotel guests wake up!"

Zahra and Faruq talked quietly as they worked.

Zahra ['zɑ:rʌ] weibl. Vorname • 8 **Latif** [lə'ti:f] Nachname • 14 **shook** [ʃʊk] schüttelte • 15 **wicked** ['wɪkɪd] bösartig • 18 **baitfish** ['beɪtfɪʃ] Köderfisch

"I don't think Dad is fishing today," said Zahra. "I'm sure that he and the other fishermen are trying to organise something – you know, to catch the criminals."

"How can they watch such a big fishing area day and night? No chance, Zahra! But you're right: We're talking about *real* criminals," said Faruq. "They're only interested in the money they get for the fish. They **stun** them here and transport them across the world. And all those people who buy the fish for their aquarium don't know. Or worse: They just don't care. Who cares if the **cyanide** they use to stun those fish also kills a lot of the other sea creatures around here! It makes me furious!"

"Ssh, Faruq!" said Zahra. "The guests may hear you. We have to get this wheelbarrow out of sight now. The hotel manager will be very angry if anyone sees it!"

"Listen, Zahra," said Faruq as she helped him push the wheelbarrow. "You know I hate to tell a lie. Well, one of the Australians asked me what fish we put in the kirugarudhiya. And I told him it was red snapper."

"That's what it is. You *didn't* lie," whispered Zahra.

"Yes," said Faruq, "but one of them suggested it came fresh from the fisherman's net ... But *we* all know that the fish in that curry was **imported**, deep frozen!"

"You didn't say that, did you?!" asked Zahra, worried.

"No, of course not: I'm not stupid," answered Faruq, "but keeping quiet, to me, is like lying!" He knew that fishing was a big problem around there and they really needed the tourists' money for their survival.

Zahra and Faruq pushed the wheelbarrow past the walkway. Not a sound came from the water villas at the other end. Behind the staff quarters a boat was waiting to collect the dead fish. Zahra took one last look at the wheelbarrow. Hundreds of cold, dead eyes **stared** back at her sadly.

7 **to stun** [stʌn] lähmen, betäuben • 10 **cyanide** [ˈsaɪənaɪd] Zyanid • 23 **to import** [ɪmˈpɔːt] einführen • 33 **stared** [steəd] starrten

Part 3 Shadows and light

Amber had slept badly. And she had a **headache**. She heard the sound of a boat in the distance. But the others were all asleep. She got up quietly to get a glass of water.

Damn this headache, she thought. She didn't want to miss the dive. She could take a **tablet**, but she needed some food in her stomach first and it was too early for breakfast.

Amber stood at the window of the living room and looked towards the island. The sun had only just come up and across the walkway she noticed shadows on the beach. Then she saw that it was Faruq with a young woman. They were talking and pushing a wheelbarrow. Suddenly they stopped and Faruq picked something up from the sand. He held it in his hand. It was a fish.

Amber couldn't understand what Faruq was saying, but she could tell that he was angry. She looked at the wheelbarrow. It was completely full, she **realised** – full of dead fish!

• • •

1 **headache** ['hedeɪk] Kopfweh • 5 **tablet** ['tæblət] (Schmerz-) Tablette • 17 **to realise** ['rɪəlaɪz] feststellen

After breakfast Amber's headache was no better.

"Joel, I've taken a tablet, but it's not much better. Abu thinks I should miss this dive," moaned Amber. "He says the pressure underwater will make the headache worse. So please lend Hayley my camera. I'll just lie in the shade, under a coconut tree, I guess, until you get back."

"Yeah, but not where coconuts could fall on your head! That wouldn't be too good for your headache," Joel joked. Then he put his hand on her arm and added quickly, "Sorry, Amber. That wasn't very funny. Hope you feel better soon!"

"I hope so, too!" said Amber and gave him a quick kiss.

But when the divers left, Amber decided to go over to the hotel spa and see if she could get a massage.

There, in the women's section, someone called Zahra offered her a cool, fresh juice cocktail. Then she took Amber into a room that smelled of flowers. The light there was friendly but not too bright. In the middle of the room was a big **bathtub** full of water and special **herbs**.

When Amber was in the tub – with her head back on a special **pillow** – Zahra began to massage her face gently.

Amber closed her eyes and tried to relax, but she **kept seeing** the dead fish. She opened her eyes again quickly.

"Zahra," she began, "maybe you can help me. Can I please ask you something?"

Zahra looked at her shyly. She must be about my age, thought Amber.

"Yes, Mrs …?" Zahra said.

"My name is Amber," she offered.

"Yes, Amber, of course you can ask – if I can help you with your problem. Is it about your headache?"

"No, it's something else," said Amber. "Maybe you know Faruq, the waiter?"

"What about him? Is there some trouble?" asked Zahra.

19 **bathtub** [ˈbɑːθtʌb] Badewanne • 19 **herbs** [hɜːbz] Kräuter • 21 **pillow** [ˈpɪləʊ] Kissen • 22 **kept seeing** [ˌkept ˈsiːɪŋ] sah immer wieder

"No, no, nothing like that," Amber assured her. "I saw him with a woman early this morning ... on the beach. They were collecting dead fish ..." She stopped when she saw how shocked Zahra looked.

"You haven't said anything to the other guests!" said Zahra.

"Well, yes, I told my boyfriend and the others in our water villa," answered Amber, "Zahra, why is the beach full of dead fish? What's happening?"

"We don't know. I wish we had some idea. I hate seeing all those dead fish!" said Zahra angrily. "My brother says, we mustn't talk to the tourists about this – we shouldn't spoil their holiday here."

"Ah, Zahra, was it *you* with Faruq?" guessed Amber. "I couldn't really see because the woman had one of those headscarves on ... So, Faruq is your brother?"

"Yes: He's my twin brother. We're 17. And you?" Zahra put her hand over her mouth. "Oh, sorry! I shouldn't ..."

"It's OK, Zahra. I'm *nearly* 17," said Amber with a smile.

The two teenagers chatted a little. Zahra gave Amber a foot massage and slowly her head stopped hurting. After she had had her shower, Amber went to the juice bar. There Zahra served her a drink and a snack. She learnt that Zahra wanted to go back to college, but the family needed her help. Fishing wasn't bringing in much money these days ...

"Hey, Zahra," said Amber. "Can I ask you one more thing?"

"Er ... I don't know about that!" said Zahra with a smile.

"Well, I'd really like a photo of us together on my mobile," laughed Amber.

"Well, ... OK. But only if you promise to send it to me!" said Zahra, "Oh, Amber ... I must get back to work now!"

Part 4 Islanders: Faruq and Zahra

Faruq was free for the rest of that day. So after Zahra had finished her work at the spa, they walked down to the **pier**. They could see Abu's boat, not too far away now.

When the divers arrived, Amber came to meet them. They all helped to get the equipment off the boat.

Then Abu called to Faruq, "You don't need a **dhoni**. I can take you and Zahra home, if you want. I'm going that way in about five minutes."

"Ah, don't you live here?" asked Zach, and smiled. Although he spoke to Faruq, his eyes were on Zahra. But she was looking past him out over the wide, open sea.

"No," answered Faruq, "not when I've got a day off!"

"Well, come on Faruq," laughed Abu, "or your free day will be over before you can say '**kurumba**'!"

On the boat Faruq turned to Zahra, "So how do you know Zach?" he asked.

"I've never met him before, Faruq," answered Zahra.

"Well, that's good. You know that you shouldn't **mix** with the tourists: Some may be OK, but they're only here for fun. They come, and then they go again!"

"That's a smart definition of *tourists* – thank you, brother dear, I'll remember that," laughed Zahra. Then suddenly, she was serious again. "One of your tourists came to the spa today. She saw us on the beach – and she saw the fish ..."

"Well, that means trouble ..." said Faruq.

"But, at least Amber promised to stay quiet about it – and I trust her," said Zahra.

"As if a girl can stay quiet about anything!" joked Faruq in a loud voice.

"Very funny! ... But tell me, *who* can't stay quiet now?!" was Zahra's quick response.

• • •

2 **pier** [ˈpɪə] Pier, Landungsbrücke • 6 **dhoni** [ˈdəʊni] ein traditionelles maledivisches Boot • 14 **kurumba** [kuːˈruːmbʌ] Kokosnuss auf Dhivehi • 18 **to mix** [mɪks] *hier:* private Kontakte pflegen

When they arrived on their fishing island, Faruq invited Abu to join them later, for dinner.

"My parents are always happy to see you, Abubakar. You haven't visited us for some time."

"OK, thanks," answered Abu, "I'll come right over after evening prayers. I think my mum made '**foni boakiba**' this morning, so I'll bring some if I can!"

"Oh, my favourite pudding!" **exclaimed** Zahra and Faruq at the same time.

Later, when they were having dinner, Abu told the Latifs' about the trip that day with the Australian tourists.

"One of the divers asked about the dead fish," said Abu.

Faruq looked at Zahra, but said nothing.

"So, Abubakar, what did you tell them?" asked Mr Latif, and put his head in his hands.

"None of us knows why they're dying – that's all I could say," explained Abu. "But then his friend, Zach, asked directly: Is it safe, for example, to brush your teeth with the **tap water** on Suvaruge Fushi?"

"And you told them about the island's water **purification** system," suggested Zahra, "so at least there's no worry about that."

"Yes, Zahra," said Abu. "But Zach is right to ask. So maybe we should just check things with one of the technical staff."

"I think he should keep his nose out of our problems, but I'll talk to one of the guys there tomorrow – just so that everyone's happy," said Faruq angrily.

"Cheer up, brother," said Zahra. Of course, they were all worried. But she hated it when her brother got so furious. "Come on, Faruq. Have some of Abu's mum's foni boakiba. It's **heavenly**! Here, try some. Maybe it'll help to make your life a bit sweeter …"

6 **foni boakiba** ['fəʊni ˌbəʊʌ'kiːbʌ] Pudding aus Reis und Kokosmilch • 8 **to exclaim** [ɪks'kleɪm] (aus-) rufen • 19 **tap water** ['tæpˌwɔːtə] Leitungswasser • 20 **purification** [ˌpjʊərɪfɪ'keɪʃn] Aufbereitungs- • 32 **heavenly** ['hevnli] himmlisch

Part 5 Underwater bird of myth

It was their fourth day in the Maldives. The diving group and an extra crew member were on board Abu's boat. Today they were on the **outer reef**. As always, it was a warm, sunny morning. But the sea wasn't as calm as the days before. Amber was glad that she didn't get seasick.

Connor felt a bit queasy, so he didn't want to dive – and Hayley decided to stay on the boat with him.

"OK, guys," said Abu, "we're visiting a **cleaning station** today. And I hope we'll see some **manta rays**. So get your camera ready, Amber. We're not diving deep – about ten metres. But the current here is very strong."

"I'd say we're up current now," guessed Zach, "so won't we hit the reef with a crash?"

"No, there's a sand channel behind some coral heads. That's where we want to land," explained Abu. "The idea is to let out all the air in your jacket, so you drop quicker than the current carries you along. Then pivot at about ten metres. That should get you to the sand channel. As I said, we're not deep, but we could be down there for some time. So your decompression stops on the way up are important. OK? Let's go!"

They went down almost together. Amber was really excited. She felt the strong current right away. It pushed her along. The others were in front of her. No! Hang on! Where was her buddy? At that moment Joel went past and dropped far below her. She began to pivot. Now she could see the sand channel. The current moved her along. Just then Joel took her hand and she pulled him with her. Together they went with a crash into the channel.

They all waited behind a couple of coral heads, which protected the divers well from the current.

---

3 **outer reef** [ˌaʊtə ˈriːf] *hier:* weiter entfernt, Außenriff • 8 **cleaning station** [ˈkliːnɪŋ ˌsteɪʃn] ein Ort im Ozean, an dem kleine Fische große putzen • 9 **manta ray** [ˈmæntə ˌreɪ] Mantarochen

Twenty minutes passed, and there wasn't a manta in sight.

Joel swam into the channel to explore the coral life there. He pointed to something, maybe to the **school** of colourful bannerfish. Amber got a shot of him as they moved around him. But then Abu banged on his **oxygen flask** and pointed, too – out of the channel and into the deep blue sea – just as a large, cloudy **shape** came out of the shadows! It was about five metres long and blue-grey. Its fins were like the wings of a fantastic huge bird out of some myth. The manta swam towards them easily, as if there was no current at all. Amber got as many shots as she could.

Soon the manta was directly above the coral head. Amber watched, surprised, as a number of smaller fish offered their services – and began to 'clean' the huge creature.

The divers weren't very deep down, but they had spent a very long time in the channel – more than an hour by now. Abu decided that it was time to go back up again.

The boat picked them up some distance away from where they had gone down. As they took off their wetsuits, the divers told Connor and Hayley all about their adventures.

"You're making me jealous," exclaimed Hayley. "I've never seen a manta before!"

"Hope you got lots of shots, Amber!" added Connor.

As they talked, Joel sat down with the logbook and wrote the day's entry – or tried to write it: He wasn't feeling too good. He couldn't think right. His body itched, his left hand felt dead and his knees hurt terribly. And it felt like his heart was running a race! Abu came over to Joel.

"Are you OK, mate?" asked Abu.

"No, er ... I feel sick ... My body hurts," said Joel weakly.

"OK, just lie down," said Abu. "You need decompression: I'll call the **dive base** for a plane to fly you out!"

4 **school** [sku:l] Schwarm • 6 **oxygen flask** ['ɒksɪdʒən ˌflɑ:sk] Sauerstoffflasche • 8 **shape** [ʃeɪp] Form, Gestalt • 34 **dive base** ['daɪv beɪs] Tauchstation

After that things happened very quickly. Amber wanted to go with Joel, but they assured her that he'd be OK. She watched the plane as it got smaller and smaller. When it was just a tiny dot in the sky, she turned to the others.

"He'll be OK, Amber," said Zach. "It's not dangerous and it's only for a day or so."

"Yes, don't worry," added Abu. "Joel **tends** to dive too deep and to come up too fast, I've noticed. Then sometimes he can't pivot right. But your buddy will be back soon, you'll see."

"Joel loves that 'diving' feeling – **me, too**. Only, I'm just a bit more careful, I guess," laughed Amber although there were tears in her eyes.

"Well, OK," said Abu, "I'll take you back to Suvaruge Fushi now: I think you all need to rest a bit."

• • •

Back on the island, Amber went straight to the spa and looked for Zahra. She found her in the juice bar.

---

7 to tend to [tend] zu etw. neigen • **11 me, too** [miː ˈtuː] ich auch

"Hi, Amber! Oh, ... what's wrong?" Zahra asked when she saw the look on her friend's face.

"Joel ..." said Amber quietly.

"Oh, Amber – OK, listen," said Zahra quietly. "The spa closes in a few minutes. Then I'm free to talk."

Later they sat in the shade behind the spa. Amber told Zahra what had happened.

"Your friend will be fine, Amber," said Zahra as she put her arm around her. "But it's good that there's a decompression chamber near here. I really don't think it's dangerous."

"That's exactly what Zach told me," said Amber, and tried to smile.

"Zach's a good diver, isn't he?" said Zahra, as she **smoothed** down her headscarf. "So he must know. Well, ... and er ... he *seems* honest ..."

"Yes, you can trust Zach, I'm sure. We only met him because he joined the diving group in Sydney. But he and Joel have become good mates now. You'd never guess that he has got such stinking rich parents: I think he's just a really nice, friendly guy ..."

"Is Zach his real name?" asked Zahra, shyly.

"No, it's Zachariya. I think his grandparents came to Australia from North India ..." Amber stopped and looked at her friend. "Hey, Zahra?"

The blood rushed to Zahra's face. "Yeah, well, ... he's ... a nice guy, just as you said. I don't really know him, do I?"

"Well, he asked about you, too – after he saw you on the pier. He wanted to know if you and Faruq are ..."

"Boyfriend and girlfriend?" laughed Zahra.

At that moment Faruq came around the corner and said, "Hi, there, Amber. Hi, **sis**. Listen, Abu has already left. But there's a dhoni on its way here – if you're quick, you'll catch it!"

---

15 to smooth down [smu:θ 'daʊn] glattstreichen • **32 sis** [sɪs] *Abkürzung von* sister

Part 6 Islanders: Faruq

Faruq walked down to the pier with Zahra. When she had left, he went over to the staff buildings.

"Hi, Murad," he said to the **technician** as he entered the lab. "Good to see you here. Have you got time for a chat?"

"Yeah, what's up?" asked Murad.

"Abu says one of the Aussies is in 'the chamber'! But the hotel manager told me to come to you: The guests are asking about our tap water. You check it regularly, I guess?"

"For cyanide? Of course," Murad said. "We're checking it all the time. With this new '**chemosensor**' technology the tiniest **amounts** show deep blue on a test **strip**."

"And if there's cyanide in the water?" asked Faruq.

"No problem: We put something into the water and the cyanide is **neutralised**." Murad looked at Faruq and added, "It's safe. Water purification is not cheap. But we really can't **afford** *not* to have it: Any mistakes would be deadly!"

"Yes – for all of us!" added Faruq. "But tell me: Any news on the cyanide fishing front?"

"The police arrested two people – in the east," reported Murad. "But on the radio they didn't say anything about the evidence."

"Well, that can't be why there are dead fish on our beach. The current doesn't **run** that way," explained Faruq and added, "OK, thanks for the info, Murad."

Faruq left the lab and walked down to the pier. He had just half an hour before he had to put on his waiter clothes and meet the guests with a friendly smile. Not a happy thought right then. OK, his job here was fine and he usually enjoyed meeting the tourists.

---

3 **technician** [tek'nɪʃn] Techniker/-in • 11 **chemosensor** ['ki:məˌsensə] Chemorezeptor • 12 **amount** [ə'maʊnt] Menge • 12 **strip** [strɪp] Streifen • 15 **to neutralise** ['nju:trlaɪz] neutralisieren • 17 **to afford** [ə'fɔ:d] leisten • 25 **to run** [rʌn] (ver-)laufen

But sometimes he just felt frustrated. For example, he would love to have his own dive school. But he didn't even have his instructor certificate. Why couldn't he have some of Zahra's **optimism**? Well, … maybe Zahra is right – maybe he should talk to Abubakar …

"Sorry to bother you: May I sit down next to you?" asked someone behind him. He turned around. It was Zach.

"Yes, of course, but I have to start work in a few minutes," answered Faruq. He didn't want to seem unfriendly.

"I have a question: You see, I've dived a lot. But you must have much more experience," started Zach.

"I don't know about that," said Faruq – but he thought: Why didn't he ask their diving instructor?

"I wanted to ask Abu," said Zach, as if he had read his thoughts. "But things happened in such a hurry today. Well, I've never had the **bends**, but I checked the **symptoms** again. Joel had some that aren't typical: His heart was racing and he couldn't think right. Later he felt dizzy. Have you ever seen symptoms like that, Faruq?"

Faruq realised that Zach was really worried about his friend. He put his hand on the young Australian's shoulder and said: "Well, no, I haven't. But your morning dive wasn't that deep, Abu told me. And you did longer decompression stops. So Joel's bends can't be that bad. And Joel is in good hands, so don't worry, Zach."

"Thanks, Faruq, you've been a great help!" said Zach and he got up to leave.

"No problem! See you later!" said Faruq.

The guy is OK, he thought, as he watched Zach walk down the pier and along to the walkway. And what *if* he likes Zahra? He hasn't even talked to her! No, he's OK …

"It's just me. I must have dead fish on the brain!" said Faruq to nobody but the sea and the sky.

---

4 **optimism** ['ɒptɪmɪzm] Optimismus • 16 **the bends** [bendz] Taucherkrankheit • 16 **symptom** ['sɪmtəm] Symptom, Krankheitserscheinung

Part 7 In the picture

Amber, Zach, Connor and Hayley entered the restaurant gardens together. None of them was hungry, but they decided not to just hang around in the villa.

Amber had called Joel. He'd said not to worry, he'd be back tomorrow. But he sounded really ill. Amber decided not to go on the wreck dive the next day but to give Joel a surprise, instead. Also, she had so many photos to sort and download. The one of Joel, **surrounded** by bannerfish, came to her head. If it's good, I'll **frame** it, she thought.

Faruq came to their table and they ordered their drinks.

"Hi, Faruq," said Zach, "one other thing I forgot to ask you about: Are you with us on tomorrow's dive?"

"Yes, Abu asked me because I know that ship better than the back of my hand," answered Faruq.

"Hey that's great, eh, Amber?" said Zach and turned to look at her. She seemed miles away.

"Sorry, Zach? The dive? Er … I think I'll just stay here, I'm not too interested in wrecks," said Amber.

"Oh! OK, Amber," said Zach. Then he turned to Faruq. "Well, then: Abu is staying on his boat, he said. So that means you and I are buddies tomorrow!"

"Great!" laughed Faruq.

• • •

Amber sat in her room. It was quite late, but she just couldn't sleep. Instead, she switched on her laptop to download the pictures of the last dive. But then she remembered that great photo of Zahra at the juice bar which she had sent to Zahra's mobile, as promised. And she decided to put it on her laptop.

"Not bad," she thought. The picture was clear enough, on the screen, although it was a bit **grainy**. There was

---

8 **surrounded** [sə'raʊndɪd] umgeben • 9 **to frame** [freɪm] einrahmen • 31 **grainy** ['greɪni] körnig

Zahra with a bright smile, as she posed sweetly for the photo. Her thick, black hair fell in waves to her shoulders.

There was a knock at her door.

"Hey, Amber, you're still up!" said Zach, looking in.

"Yes, but you, too," she said.

"Oh, I went for a long walk on the beach – I'm trying to sort my thoughts ..." explained Zach. Then he stopped suddenly. "Hey!" he said, surprised. "That's Zahra! Wow!"

"Is that 'Wow, Amber: What a great photo'? – or is it: 'Wow, isn't that Zahra beautiful'? Now, Zach, be careful how you answer!" joked Amber.

"Well, to be honest, both!" said Zach. Then he added, "Well, I don't know Zahra at all, but I think there's something special about her ..."

"But, Zach, I don't think Zahra is the **holiday romance** type," said Amber.

"I know. Maybe that's why I like her," said Zach quietly.

"Is that what you were thinking about on your walk?" asked Amber softly.

"Well, not only that," answered Zach slowly. "We're all leaving in a few days. And I thought of Joel – how he'll miss the wreck dive tomorrow. But, back home I've also got a problem: My dad expects me to become a dentist ..."

"And *you*? What do *you* want?" asked Amber.

"I'd be happiest on an island like this one. I'd love to open a dive school, or something. But tell my dad that!"

"Well, you said that your dad's a businessman: A dive school is a business. So Zach: Like father like son. You'll just have to *sell* the idea to him!"

"You don't know my dad," Zach **sighed**. "Thanks, it's a help to chat. Amber – can you send me that photo?"

"I don't know, Zach, er ... maybe," said Amber, and smiled.

• • •

15 holiday romance [ˌhɒlədeɪ rəʊˈmæns] Urlaubsliebe • **30 to sigh** [saɪ] seufzen

The next morning the diving group left at the crack of dawn. Amber waited on the pier with tears in her eyes. Zahra arrived in her dad's fishing boat half an hour later.

"Listen, I must talk to you," said Amber, **sobbing**. "I just got a call from Joel's dad. He flew out from Sydney. He's with Joel now. They've moved him to a different hospital! The doctors there say that it's something else – not just the bends. Oh, Zahra, I should have gone with him! I must get to him quickly!"

"Oh, no, Amber! Just go to reception. They'll sort it out for you," said Zahra. "Did his dad say what's wrong?"

"No, but they **pumped out** his stomach last night. And they're doing lots of blood tests. Joel's dad thinks maybe it's **poisoning**!" said Amber.

A horrible idea flashed into Zahra's head. She put her hand to her mouth. Cyanide, she thought, shocked. She tried to remember her brother's exact words that morning – when she helped him with the dead fish: 'Who cares if the cyanide they use to stun those fish also kills …'!

"Amber, Joel's dad might be right," said Zahra carefully. "Listen, you have to call him *now* and say that it could be cyanide poisoning. He must tell the doctors really fast!"

Amber called him and passed on the information. Then Zahra explained how and why fish are stunned.

Amber thought back to her last dive with Joel.

"No, Zahra," she started, "how can that be? Joel and I – and the others – did every dive *together*. If he got cyanide poisoning, then we would all have it, too! But let's think … What about the food, here at the hotel? The fish is caught locally, right? So maybe …"

Now the secret is out, thought Zahra. "No, Amber. With the problem of those dead fish, the hotel manager didn't want to take any risks. The fish is not fresh – and not local either."

4 **sobbing** ['sɒbɪŋ] schluchzend • 12 **to pump out** [pʌmp 'aʊt] auspumpen • 14 **poisoning** ['pɔɪznɪŋ] Vergiftung

"Good. OK, so let's still say it *is* poisoning. Then, what we have to **work out** is: Why haven't we all got it, too?"

"Yes, you're right," said Zahra. "But, Amber, I'm sorry – I have to open the spa now. Three or four women have booked massages after breakfast ... But we must talk before you fly out there!"

So Amber left Zahra and walked towards the main building. She tried to remember the details of that last dive. Suddenly she stopped and turned away at the door.

If I leave now, thought Amber, how can I find out what's going on? Joel could be in real danger! She quickly pushed that idea out of her head. Oh, Joel! What should I do?

But she knew the answer already: She shouldn't fly to Joel. She had to solve the mystery before it was too late!

• • •

Amber sat on the sofa, staring at her laptop screen.

"Hi! More shots of Zahra?" Zach asked as he came in.

2 to work out [wɜːk ˈaʊt] herausfinden

“No, Zach. Look, what’s that down there?” Amber pointed to a strange shape, only partly **visible**.

“Well, I can’t really say because there’s only a small bit of it in the shot,” answered Zach. “But look at that line along there: It’s really very straight. I don’t think it can be a fish or some coral …”

“Exactly!” exclaimed Amber.

“Oh … OK, Amber,” said Zach. “I don’t really know what you mean. So what do you think it is?”

Zach stood up and looked around. “Hey, wait a minute! Where’s Joel? Isn’t he back yet?” Zach asked, surprised.

“No, he’s worse, Zach. His dad called from the hospital,” said Amber. “He sounded really worried.”

She told Zach the details – and what she knew from Zahra.

“I can’t believe it! Cyanide?!” exclaimed Zach. “But we were all down there together, so how can that be?”

“Well,” said Amber. “It can’t be cyanide from stunning. But it must have something to do with that sand channel.”

“Well,” said Zach, “that just means that we have to go back down there again – and get a closer look.”

“No, Zach,” said Amber, “not a *closer* look: A better look – from a safe distance, and with the right camera **lens**!”

“OK, you’re right. It wouldn’t help Joel if we all got sick! Look, I’ll go and talk to Abu now before he goes home,” said Zach. “I think he’s still down on the pier, with Faruq and the others. I only came in to tell you that we’re back!”

“OK, I’m going over to the spa. I promised to tell Zahra what we’re planning. If she’s free, maybe she can come with us. She’s worried, too, you know. I’ll join you all in about ten minutes,” said Amber as she hurried out.

2 visible [ˈvɪzəbl] sichtbar • **24 lens** [lens] Linse

Part 8 Islanders: Zahra and Faruq

Later, in her afternoon break, Zahra stood in the shade behind the spa with Faruq. She hated arguments with her brother – but now they were in the middle of a big one.

"Listen, Faruq," she said in a calmer voice. "It sounds really dangerous to me. But Amber says she can get the shot from a distance with a special camera lens. And Abu said yes to Amber. I know that he won't take any risks when he's down there with them …"

"Of course not: He's responsible for the tourists' **safety**," shouted Faruq. "You're not a diver: So the dive boat is no place for you – with or without Amber!"

"But she's my friend! I *must* be there. Please, Faruq: If you say yes, Abu will let me come!" said Zahra.

"Well, what about your work?" asked Faruq. "You know, you can't just **cancel** your **appointments**."

Ah, thought Zahra, he's softening. It's good that I've already swapped my free day with the other girl! But she said sweetly, "I'm free tomorrow … Oh, come on, Faruq!"

Just then Abu came around the corner.

"Hi, there, you two," said Abu. "Faruq, it's just us two with Zach and Amber tomorrow. The other couple, Hayley and Connor, are doing the fishing village tour."

Zahra stared at her brother and thought: Aha! So it looks like they really could need my help …

"Abu," said Faruq, "Zahra wants to be on the boat with me, if that's OK with you?"

"Why not?" smiled Abu. "Extra crew might be useful!"

"Thanks, Abu," said Zahra, "I'll meet you all on the pier at dawn. Bye, Abu. See you later, Faruq."

As she spoke, she gave her brother one of her sunniest smiles. Then she turned and went back into the spa to her waiting guests.

---

9 **safety** [ˈseɪfti] Sicherheit • 15 **to cancel** [ˈkænsl] absagen • 15 **appointment** [əˈpɔɪntmənt] Termin

Part 9 Back to the sand channel

On the way to the reef Zahra said, "The police let those two fishermen go. There was no real evidence. Dad was glad. He can't believe that any of our local fishermen are responsible. We all **live off** the sea, he says: We only catch fish to eat! Poisoning the water is deadly for all of us!"

"He's right," said Amber.

"Yes, people have learnt from the past," said Faruq. "You know, many years ago fish stunning was quite normal in the Maldives."

"So how did that change?" asked Zach.

"Well, there were big **campaigns** against it. And the officials made the laws stricter," answered Faruq.

"Also, the fishing communities kept their eyes open and reported anything strange," added Zahra. "Then when the police caught any criminals, they put them in prison *and* gave them really high fines."

"But, what about all those dead fish?" Amber asked.

"Oh, that only began about three weeks before you all arrived," said Faruq. "There were no local reports of stunning around our islands before that!"

Abu stopped the boat and they prepared for the dive.

Amber, Zach and Abu went down. They reached the channel together. But this time no one was interested in the underwater life there.

Amber held her camera in her hands. She was standing exactly in the same place as last time – when she had taken that photo of Joel. Zach and Abu were not far behind her. Now, she moved on just a bit until she was around the side of a long coral head. She turned slowly **to face** where Joel had pointed that day.

Now, finally, she knew what Joel had seen: There, directly in the reef, was a big metal **drum**!

4 **to live off** [lɪv ˈɒf] sich ernähren von • 11 **campaign** [kæmˈpeɪn] Kampagne • 29 **to face** [feɪs] den Blick auf … richten • 32 **drum** [drʌm] Fass

The other two waited for Amber to get some shots. It was nearly the same scene, but without Joel. That felt kind of scary ... And now her hands were shaking so much that she found it hard to hold the camera **still**. Then she remembered: Joel is really ill – we're down here for him! That helped her to become calmer.

Soon she stopped shaking and got some good shots. Then she **backed away** carefully. A few minutes later, she gave them the thumbs-up signal. They began to swim up again.

Faruq and Zahra collected them and, as they all hurried back to the island, the divers told them what they had found.

Amber downloaded the photos onto her laptop as soon as she got back to the villa. They all stood around her, **eager** to find out more about the drum and its contents.

4 **still** [stɪl] ruhig • 8 **to back away** [ˌbæk əˈweɪ] zurückweichen • 16 **eager** [ˈiːgə] eifrig

Amber had one of the photos up on the screen. She started **to magnify** it.

"Look that's the poison symbol!" exclaimed Zach, as he pointed to the **skull** and **bones** on the drum. "You can't see the other sign clearly: Could that thing there be a tree?"

"Maybe, but those numbers are probably most important," said Abu. "Maybe they're an international code for dangerous goods, or something like that!"

"Oh, my God!" said Amber. "We still don't know what the poison is!"

"No, and the drum has a leak," said Zach. "There's no time to lose! We must tell the police! I think we should e-mail the photos to them now – and to the hospital: They need to know what the poison is so they can **treat** Joel!"

"You're right, Zach," said Zahra. "The lab there will know what the numbers mean. Just ring Joel's dad and explain it all. That would be quickest, I think."

Amber followed Zahra's suggestion right away and called Joel's dad: He was sitting next to his son's bed. Joel was on a **drip**. And they also gave him **oxygen**. He was awake, but his mind was sometimes a bit foggy and he was quite short of breath. The doctors told him he must just rest and try not to talk. They were still doing tests.

Amber told Joel's dad about the drum – and about the code numbers, which might help them to find the poison quicker.

"Please give lots of love to Joel from me – from all of us!" said Amber. "I'll text you the code because there are quite a lot of numbers. OK. Bye, Mr Thompson!"

Then Amber wrote the following message:

```
Hello, Mr Thompson. Here's the code:
CAS #:143-33-9; EINECS: 205-599-4; UN 1689
```

2 to magnify [ˈmæɡnɪfaɪ] vergrößern • **4 skull** [skʌl] Totenkopf • **4 bone** [bəʊn] Knochen • **14 to treat** [triːt] behandeln • **20 drip** [drɪp] Tropf, Infusion • **20 oxygen** [ˈɒksɪdʒən] Sauerstoff

"Joel's dad will check his mobile and take the code to the hospital lab right now!" said Amber. "He'll call back as soon as he can." Then she gave them all an update on Joel's **condition**.

"Now they'll have those code numbers," said Abu. "So I'm sure that they'll get Joel on his feet again in no time!"

"Righty-ho, Amber. You know what they say: You can't keep a good man down! So cheer up!" added Zach.

"I think lunch might help. It's after 12 o'clock," said Faruq suddenly. "And it's a long time since we had that coconut water on the boat!"

"Maybe we can eat lunch together," said Zach. "When does your work start, Faruq?"

"Not till 6 pm," he answered.

"But none of the staff can eat in the hotel bars or restaurants," said Zahra.

"Hang on!" said Faruq. "Maybe we can all have lunch at our place. I'll call home and ask Mum!"

"We can't do that," said Amber. "That's five of us, Faruq – your mum will go crazy!"

"No, she won't," Zahra assured her friend. "That's part of our tradition. People just **drop in**. And they can't leave with an empty stomach!"

"Thank you for the invitation, Faruq," said Zach. "It would be great to come to your home. But I have an idea. We'll call reception and order a picnic lunch. Then we have something to offer, too. What do you say to that, buddy?"

Faruq smiled and said, "Well, so I'm not the only one with good ideas around here!"

"**Bighead**!" exclaimed Amber and Zahra together.

"OK, guys," said Abu, "I'm hungry! And all your dive equipment is still on board. Come on, let's order that food, then get the stuff off the boat – and leave!"

4 **condition** [kən'dɪʃn] Zustand • 22 **to drop in** [drɒp 'ɪn] vorbeikommen • 30 **bighead** ['bɪghed] Angeber/-in

Part 10 Islanders and tourists

On the boat Abu called the **marine** police and gave them the exact bearings for the sunken drum and the code details of its deadly content. He told them about Joel's condition – which clearly pointed to a leak.

"Yes, of course," said Abu into his mobile, "I'll e-mail you a full report – and attach the photos. Yes, just call me when your dive team is ready to go out there. I know exactly where the drum is. Tomorrow! Oh, OK! Bye." He ended the call and turned to talk to Zach and Zahra who were with him at the **stern** end.

Faruq **steered** the boat with Amber at his side. As they came nearer to the fishing island, she took some photos.

"There are about 200 people in our village. So everyone knows everyone," laughed Faruq. "And there are no tourists on our island. They normally need special permission to visit local islands."

"Well, what about Hayley and Connor's tour today?" asked Amber. "They're visiting a fishing village!"

"Well, that's a 'model' village for tourists, that's different." said Faruq. "This is the 'real thing' …"

"But we don't have any special permission for this trip, Faruq. So won't we – and you – get in trouble?" asked Amber, worried.

"Well, Amber," answered Faruq. "Think about it: Are you visiting us today as tourists – or as friends? There's a big difference. Our private life is not for the tourists. But our doors are always open to friends."

When they got to the Latifs' small house in the village, Zahra and Faruq's mum came out to welcome them. There were so many people – neighbours and family – there, too. They had heard about the guests and all arrived with gifts of flowers, fish snacks, sweets or fruit.

---

1 marine [mə'ri:n] Wasser- • **10 stern** [stɜ:n] Heck • **11 to steer** [stɪə] lenken

There wasn't enough space in the house, so they moved the picnic to the beach, under a group of trees.

"See?" whispered Zahra to Amber and Zach, "You didn't need to order all that hotel food!"

"This reminds me of home," said Zach. "It's just like that, too, with our family in Sydney. But part of the tradition is to bring a gift, like your neighbours and relatives, right?"

Later, Mr Latif arrived home with the other fishermen and they joined the picnic party. After they had eaten, they **fetched** their drums and other **percussion** instruments and started a session of '**bodu beru**' – a traditional song and dance on the islands. As the singer performed, the others all clapped or chanted the refrain. And the song got louder and louder until it ended in a **frenzy** of drums.

"Those drums are cool!" said Zach.

"They're made from coconut wood," explained Zahra.

"And from manta ray **skins** – they're very old!" added Faruq. "But, folks, I must go now. There's a dhoni …"

Abu offered to take Faruq back to Suvaruge Fushi. Zach and Amber decided to join them. The islanders were friendly, but it was their first visit and they didn't want to stay too long …

• • •

It was their last evening on Suvaruge Fushi. Amber sat down at the table and said hello to her friends. Just then her mobile rang. She walked out of the garden to take the call. It was Joel's dad.

So, now they knew what was in the drum: It *was* cyanide! But it wasn't the kind that they used for stunning. Luckily, Joel's condition was now **stable**. So in the morning they could fly him home to a special hospital in Sydney!

Amber finished the conversation with Mr Thompson and went back to tell the others the good news.

---

10 **to fetch** [fetʃ] holen • 10 **percussion** [pəˈkʌʃn] Schlag- • 11 **bodu beru** [ˈbɒdu: ˈberu:] „big drum" auf Dhivehi • 14 **frenzy** [ˈfrenzi] Ekstase • 17 **skin** [skɪn] Haut • 29 **stable** [ˈsteɪbl] stabil

Part 11 Departures

Nobody liked departures, especially not from Suvaruge Fushi, thought Amber. It was fantastic on the island. And she felt warm and happy when she thought of her new islander friends. But she couldn't wait to see Joel again. She smiled a little as she wondered about Zach and Zahra. She knew from Zahra that they'd exchanged numbers …

"G'day to you!" said Zach as he came out of his room with his luggage. "Amber? You know that photo of …"

"The **sunken** drum?" **teased** Amber. "What about it?"

"Hey, mate, you know what I mean!" answered Zach. "I asked for a photo and Zahra said I should ask you."

"Which one do you want?" laughed Amber.

"You've got more shots?" asked Zach, clearly confused.

Well, I don't want to be too mean, she thought – so she added quickly, "I got good shots of you two on the boat and on our picnic. I'll put them on a CD for you, OK?"

"Righty-ho, thanks a lot!" said Zach. He turned to look out of the window. "I've decided to tell my dad. I don't want to become a dentist. Let's hope he'll understand …"

Amber put her hand on his shoulder and said, "I really wish you all the luck in the world, Zach."

"Thanks. I'll need it! … One other thing, Amber," said Zach. "Back in Sydney, can I please join you at the hospital? I really want to see Joel …"

"Of course, Zach," said Amber. "I'm sure Joel would be really glad to see you, too. You must visit him! … But let's keep it a surprise, OK?"

Zach and Amber met the others on the pier to wait for the dhoni. Amber went and stood next to Zahra. Each put an arm on the other's shoulder. They looked out at the sea in silence. The water **glistened** in the early morning light of the equatorial sun.

---

9 sunken ['sʌŋkən] gesunken • **9 to tease** [ti:z] necken • **31 to glisten** ['glɪsn] glitzern

Part 12 Epilogue: Deep, blue and deadly

A few weeks later, back in Sydney, Amber sat at her desk. Joel lay on her bed as Amber checked her e-mails.

"There's one from Zahra!" she said excitedly – and clicked on it. "Oh, all it says is: Hi Amber, read this!" she said.

"Well, has she attached something?" asked Joel.

"No, it's an Internet link," she answered. "Hey, Joel, come and look at this!"

About us | Language | Newsflash | Reports | Contact us

Maldives Messenger

Deep, blue and deadly

Male. Today's police report is about a highly dramatic **strike** against international criminals who are using our waters as a **chemical dump**! Mr Abubakar Sharma, dive instructor of many years' experience, led the marine police to a drum in a local reef. This wasn't any old fisherman's drum: It was full of deadly cyanide, and there was already a leak! After a dive a tourist – Mr Joel Thompson of Sydney, Australia – became ill and landed in hospital. Through the brave action of his dive buddies, Amber **Morley** and Zach **Nourie** (both also from Sydney), they found out about the drum and informed the police. Ms Morley noticed the key clue in one of her underwater photos and passed it to the police: International code numbers on the drum showed its contents. So the doctors could treat Mr Thompson quickly.

Then the police found more numbers that weren't visible in the photos. These numbers are part of the international shipping code and they led directly to a metal production company in Europe. It seems that, on the way to the official dump, these criminals often drop drums into the ocean because it's cheaper! One such drums landed on our reef. The police have now arrested three people who will have lots of questions to answer!

---

epilogue ['epɪlɒg] Epilog, Nachwort • 8 **messenger** ['mesɪndʒə] Kurier • 10 **strike** [straɪk] Schlag • 11 **chemical dump** [ˌkemɪkl 'dʌmp] Müllhalde für Chemikalien • 17 **Morley** ['mɔːli] Nachname • 17 **Nourie** ['nuːri] Nachname

Exercises

1 On Suvaruge Fushi

a) *Find out about the group who are on holiday:*

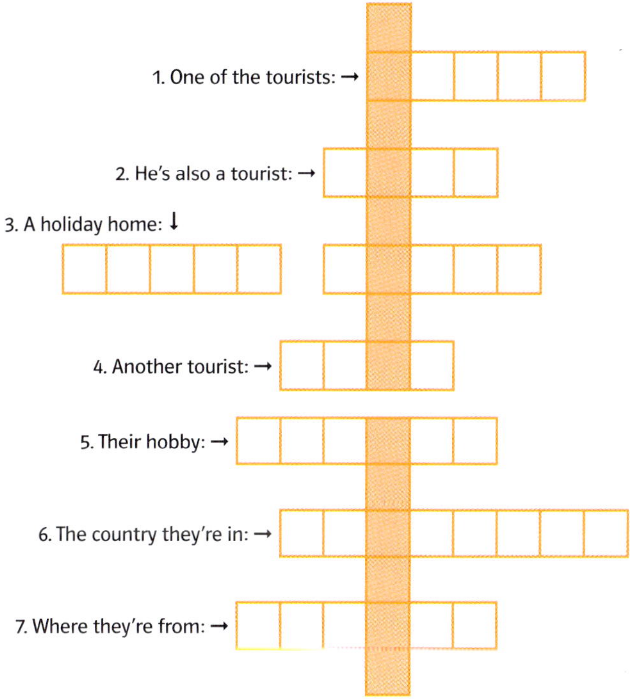

b) *Put in the missing letters to get what the tourists all feel about Suvaruge Fushi:*
They all feel it's a … .

c) *What are the names of the other two members of the group?*

d) *Who are Abubakar and Faruq? What are their jobs?*

2 Sea life

a) *The guests have fish curry for dinner (part 1, p. 9, l. 1–13). What do you learn about this curry and the fish in it?*

b) *What sea life do the teenagers see on their dive the next day? Start a mind map. Add more info as you read on.*

c) *Amber has her own diver's diary. What might she put in it after their dive (p. 10–11)? Write the entry for her. Think about the things she saw and how she felt.*

3 Just before dawn

a) *In part 2 and at the beginning of part 3 you have the same scene from the* ***islander's*** *and the* ***tourist's*** *point of view*[1]*. Make a grid. Put the words under the right heading. (Some can go under more than one heading.)*

hates lies • slept badly • shocked • furious • watching scene • head hurts • Faruq • heavy heart • Amber • collecting dead fish • worried • sees shadows • Zahra • needs tourists' money

b) *What reason does Faruq give for the dead fish?*

4 Which islander?

Look back at parts 1–4. Which islander is it – Faruq, Zahra, Mr Latif or Abu? Which lines tell you this?

1. This islander works in the spa.
2. This person knows what's in the fish curry.
3. This islander has a 'fishy' buddy!
4. This person tells the divers about the 'red list'.
5. This person has a twin brother.
6. This person isn't fishing in the area now.
7. One of the divers asks this person for help.
8. This islander's mother made a great dessert.

1 **point of view** [ˌpɔɪnt əv ˈvjuː] Erzählperspektive

5 Difficult questions

a) *Read page 18 again and find what the divers ask Abu about (two things). What answers does Abu give?*

b) *You're a hotel guest and you hear about the dead fish. Write a dialogue between you and the hotel manager and act it out in class.*

6 Diving days

a) *Read about the divers' fourth day at the beginning of part 5 (p. 19–20, down to l. 25). Compare this scene to the scene of their dive on the second day (p. 10).*

b) *Here are bannerfish, a Napoleon wrasse, a white-face butterfly fish and a manta ray. Which is which? Check on the Internet.*

a

b

c

d

c) *Which kind of fish did …*

1. … the divers see at a cleaning station?
2. … Amber take photos of on the first day?
3. … Abu say was a good friend?
4. … Amber get a shot of with Joel?

7 Faruq and tourists

a) *Read to the end of part 4, p. 18. What does Faruq think of tourists like Zach? Find the lines which tell you this.*

b) *Read on to the end of part 6. How does Faruq's opinion change? Suggest reasons for this change.*

8 Clues and links

a) *Read part 7 and look at the picture at the bottom of page 28. What is Amber showing Zach on her laptop? What do you think?*

b) *Why do the friends decide that they have to call the hospital really fast? What is the important link and who makes it?*

c) *Amber is very worried about Joel and doesn't know what to do – to fly to the hospital or to stay and try to find out more. You are Zach/Zahra. Advise her about what to do.*

9 The twins' argument

a) *Read part 8. What does 'softening' on l. 16 mean? What do you think? Check in a dictionary.*

b) *Correct these sentences.*

1. Zahra hates talking with her brother.
2. Zahra wants to take photos on the boat.
3. Faruq thinks that a hotel is no place for her.
4. But Zahra wants to be there because Zach is her friend.
5. Faruq tells her that she can't just cancel her holiday.
6. Hayley and Connor are going on the dive, too.
7. Faruq asks Abu if Zahra can fish, too.

8. Abu thinks that extra crew might be a problem.
9. So Zahra decides to meet them all after their dive.
10. And she gave her twin one of her angriest looks!

c) *What do you think of the twins' relationship*[1] *with each other? Find some examples of situations in the story to support your point of view.*

10 Evidence

a) *Read part 9. Look at these words from p. 31:*

> **police have no evidence • had big campaigns • give high fines • live off the sea • make stricter laws • catch criminals • not responsible • fish only for food • put criminals in prison • poisoning deadly for them**

b) *Make a grid for 'officials' and 'local community'. Put the words from a) under the right heading.*

c) *Why are the islanders sure that the local people aren't responsible for poisoning the water? The words in your grid can help you.*

d) *Look back at your answer to ex. 1 b) on page 4 of your reader. Did you guess right?*

e) *What do the friends do as soon as they solve the mystery? (at least three things)*

11 It's all in the news

a) *Read parts 7 and 9 again carefully and collect information about the mystery around Joel's symptoms and the results of his friends' dive.*

b) *You're a newspaper reporter for the 'Maldives Messenger' and want to interview Abubakar about the diving 'accident' and the metal drum. Think of questions to ask (Who? What? Where? When? Why?).*

1 **relationship** [rɪˈleɪʃnʃɪp] Beziehung

c) *Write a report about how the divers solved the mystery.*

d) *Read the epilogue (part 12, p. 38). What new pieces of information do you find out from the article?*

12 And then ...

a) *Think about Amber, Joel, Zach, Abu, Zahra and Faruq. Who will stay in contact with whom? Why do you think this?*

b) *What did you think of the story? Discuss what you liked or what you didn't think was good about it.*

13 Three years later

Three years later Zach opens a dive shop on Suvaruge Fushi. He has been in contact with Zahra since he left the island. Write a dialogue about the first time Zach meets Zahra and Faruq again. Start like this:

FARUQ: Hi Zach. It's so good to see you!
ZACH: Hi, you two – great to see you!
ZAHRA: ...

14 Project activities

1. A talk: All about diving

a) *What do you find out about diving in the story? Collect all the information and facts in a mind map.*

b) *Find out more about e.g. equipment, how/where (not) to dive, diving and the environment, international diving signals and rules, decompression etc. Look for useful pictures and diagrams for a more interesting presentation.*

2. A holiday brochure: Come to the Maldives!

a) *What could make the Maldives attractive to tourists? Look through the story and collect all the information about the Maldives you can find to support your answer. Make a list of the important points.*

b) *Make up the name of a Maldivian island. Look for good photo material (travel agent, magazines, Internet …). Design an attractive holiday brochure for this island.*

3. A poster: From dream to disaster?

a) *What environmental problems can people have who live by the sea? Look through the story and collect ideas.*

b) *Look for suitable photos (brochures from environmental organisations e.g. Greenpeace, magazines, Internet, …).*

c) *Think of a slogan and good captions and design a poster about environmental problems to do with the sea.*

Solutions

Before you read the story

1 The title and the cover a), b) –

2 Eco-thrillers

a) –

b) 2. An eco-thriller is kind of mystery to do with the environment.

3 Islands in paradise?

a) –

b) Main industry: tourism; then comes fishing

c) 1. An atoll is an island made of coral.
2. It forms a ring around water in the sea.
3. The name comes from the Dhivehi word 'atholhu'.
4. An atoll has small islands and reefs.
5. The atoll with the most islands is in the Maldives.

4 Diving

a) –

b) 1. mask 2. jacket 3. torch 4. buddy 5. tank 6. wetsuit 7. fin

c) 1. Let's go down. 2. I need help. 3. You OK? 4. Let's go up.

d) –

Exercises

1 On Suvaruge Fushi

a) 1. AMBER 2. ZACH 3. WATER VILLA 4. JOEL 5. DIVING 6. MALDIVES 7. SYDNEY

b) PARADISE ISLAND

c) Connor, Hayley

d) They are people from the Maldives. They work on the island: Abubakar is a diver, Faruq a waiter in the hotel.

2 Sea life

a) The fish curry is called 'kirugarudhiya'. This is a yellow coconut curry. The fish in it is red snapper (called 'Jacks' in Australia). All the guests love this curry.

b) Sea life: corals, sponges, different fish, plants, Napoleon wrasse, …

c) –

3 Just before dawn

a) *Islander's point of view:* Faruq – hates lies, furious, collecting dead fish, needs tourists' money; Zahra – shocked, heavy heart, needs tourists' money, worried; *Tourist's point of view:* Amber – slept badly, watching scene, head hurts, sees shadows

b) Cyanide fishing: Criminals stun fish to catch them and then sell them to people who want fish for their aquarium.

4 Which islander?

1. Zahra (p. 15, l. 15)
2. Faruq (p. 9, l. 5)
3. Abu (p. 11, l. 8–9)
4. Faruq (p. 11, l. 13)
5. Zahra (p. 12, l. 2)
6. Mr Latif (p. 12, l. 11)
7. Zahra (p. 15, l. 24)
8. Abu (p. 18, l. 6)

5 Difficult questions

a) One diver asks about the dead fish. Abu says that none of them knows why the fish are dying. Zach asks if it's safe to brush your/his teeth with the tap water. Abu tells him about the island's purification system.

b) –

6 Diving days

a) p. 10: soft blue, many colours, beautiful fish (nice atmosphere), p. 19/20: sea is not so calm, Connor feels queasy, strong current, … (danger)

b), c) a. white-face butterfly fish (2.), b. bannerfish (4.), c. Napoleon wrasse (3.), d. manta ray (1.)

7 Faruq and tourists

a) Faruq thinks Zach should keep his nose out of their problems (p. 18, l. 26). He's worried about Zahra and Zach.

b) Faruq notices that Zach is really worried about his friend. He realises there is no evidence for Zach's feelings for Zahra. etc.

8 Clues and links

a) –

b) Joel's poisoning could be cyanide. Zahra makes the link: She remembers what her brother said about stunning.

c) –

9 The twins' argument

a) 'Softening' means 'becoming soft'. Here it means Faruq may say yes, so Zahra continues her arguments.

b) 1. Zahra hates *arguments* with her brother. 2. Zahra wants to *come/go* on the boat. 3. Faruq thinks that *the dive boat* is no place for her. 4. But Zahra wants to be there because *Amber* is her friend. 5. Faruq tells her that she can't just cancel her *appointments*. 6. Hayley and Connor are going *to a fishing village*. 7. Faruq asks Abu if Zahra can *go/come*, too. 8. Abu thinks that extra crew might be *useful*. 9. So Zahra decides to meet them *on the pier (at dawn)*. 10. And she gave her twin one of her *sunniest* looks!

c) They like each other and trust each other (p. 13); Faruq feels responsible for Zahra (p. 30); …

10 Evidence

a) –

b) **'officials'**: give high fines, police have no evidence, make stricter laws, catch criminals, put criminals in prison
'local community': live off the sea, had big campaigns, not responsible, fish only for food, poisoning deadly for them

c), d) –